In Case The Morning Comes

Poems

Kathy Kroener

Publisher Information

EBook Bakery

www.ebookbakery.com

email: jagche1@aol.com

ISBN 978-1-938517-88-4

© 2019 by Kathy Kroener

Preface

Dear Reader;

Dip into these poems. I hope you find some that speak to you.

Thank you for reading them and making them a part of yourself.

Kathy Kroener

Acknowledgments

Thanks to Michael of Ebook Bakery books and to my fellow poets who inspire me and to my husband, my love.

Dedication

To Mother with my love,
a true connoisseur of words and all things nature.

Poems

In memorial to my dear husband,
George Kroener, "my Che".
Aug.14, 1938 - Jan. 2, 2019

To my husband

It has been a week now my love,
an entire long week without you.
I have cried my gallons of tears,
accepted condolences, taken care
of what I can, the way you would,
the way you always did my love.

You were so steady my dear one,
so steady, and always just so here.
I'm sure that you tried to stay for me
as long as you possibly could.
How I wish I could thank you for that.
But you were so tired, I know this.
Your lungs, your heart, and kidneys.
Yes, I know that you had to go.

Yet I feel lost without you, my Che.
Therefore I cling to this rock I have.
Today, right this minute, faith tells me
that you are in a wonderful place.
Strong and healthy, well once again.
So now, my dear one take hold of
the eternal life you were called to,
and know my Che, I love you forever.

Despite the sadness

A sense of all we had and lost.
The memory of passions that died.
An awareness of increasing pain.
All the everything we must give up.
People endure such trouble and hardship.
Cry the entire human family.
Restless and wanting, sad and sick,
like a bird locked in some dark cage.

We long for freedom and for light,
yet do not know what they truly are.
We crave acceptance, and ache for love,
but so many never can find it.

Sing a song of the dreaming,
this thing that has somehow kept us alive,
and given us reason to struggle on,
despite the sadness we carry.
And sing a song of creating.
That little bit of what God does.
One tiny voice crying out loud,
"I am, I am here, and I am alive."

Uplifting

It would be a splendid thing
to write about positive matters.
Love, joy or peace, things like that.
I write all this dubious stuff.
Others who do this poetry bit,
consider more uplifting subjects
in many of the poems they make.
A baby's hand, smooth and pudgy.
Memories of a mother's love.
A grandchild's first tricycle,
or a long lost, favorite dog.

My stuff is dark, curmudgeonly,
sarcastic, sad, sometimes harsh.
I write about stones, lizards or loss,
and empty, lonely horizon nonsense.
Heavy, dismal, oppressive things.
But when I read them people laugh,
though they are not meant to be funny.
At a recent poetry presentation
the room erupted in laughter.
I had to wait till they were done
so I could finish reading my piece,
which really was about aging and pain.

It is enough to make me wonder,
if I could write cheery, light and bright,
would I give everyone reason to cry?

Vulture roost

Dozens return every evening
circling gracefully round, around.
They silently land on great branches,
that sigh and droop with a weight of birds.
Rustling wings they adjust their pinions,
as perched, they hunch to welcome the night.
What are the secret things they dream,
these lords of the effortless floating?
They've soared all day balancing, tipsing,
on thermals only a raptor could find.
People watch them with dread and fear,
a few, less commonly, worship and awe.
The roosting vultures are unconcerned,
and peacefully rest, whiling hours away.
In morning light, rousing one by one,
the birds shiver and shake their great wings.
They fling off from dark, black feathers,
thousands of glistening dew drops,
that glitter like scattered diamonds,
to arc, flash and fall in a rising sun.

Wax

It was in a basement,
musty with mold and dust.
Dirt floors, rough stone walls
chilly, festooned with webs.

A memory of a girl
huddled over the flame
of a guttering candle.
A sort of cave under the stairs,
smoke in her eyes and face.
She had crayons and wires
and blobs of pale wax.

Day after solitary day
she spent hours down there,
out of sight, out of mind.
By herself, while the others,
brother, sisters, they played
loud and boisterous games
outdoors in the sunshine,
as typical kids like to do.

Not this reclusive child.
She truly did want to be
alone in the dank, damp, dark.
She melted and formed that wax
into ephemeral figurines.
Fantastical little amulets.
Her secret creations,
that no one else would ever see.

I can remember that girl.
But I do wish I could recall
those fragile things that she made.
They were so carefully done,
and so important at the time.

Wander songs

In some far off place
which one is that one
tell that wanderer
you must own your pain
and learn what you are
to hitch down that long
long and winding road
to touch the horizon
of some lonely sea
to stand on the black rocks
and let that self go
sink deep and drowning
as the cold cold water
surrounds you now
and all you have got
is this trembling hand

DRAG

I feel strange
empty somehow
wrung out used up
a wet towel
twisted and squeezed
torqued nearly torn
slung carelessly
over some fence
to hang there limp
in scorching sun

Widdershins

She wanders about her life,
a daughter of discord.
Widdershins in everything.
So don't follow her unless
you wish to find yourself lost.
She could lead you as far as
a place the gray sea knows,
her grayer stone house in woods.
She might even lure you down
to the edge of that forbidden line,
where the darkness touches light
and the twisted root has voice.
A black raven one that she keeps
will croak and rasp in your ear,
to provide you with song in the night.
Her crystals can dazzle your eyes
so you never will find your way home.
Too, she's apt to weave viney things
into the tangles of your silver hair,
as she whispers to you her secrets
of love and loneliness and loss.

Plop

Some long ago farm pond
I would guess that this was.
Now, just a brief rest stop
along the quiet trail
of this nature preserve.
I see several turtles
basking in the sun, warm,
hauled out along the edge.
The bigger ones, snappers
I must assume, lurk below.
I'll tickle the surface
with a long stem of grass
and lure one to rise slow,
trailing bubbles from dark mud.
A real prehistoric thing
I wonder what it knows?
A night heron crouches there
on an overhang branch.
While a big, green bullfrog
slips off a lily pad,
and in with a modest plop.

Wants to

She just wants to
pick a thing up
examine it
and put it back
choose another
bead or button
shiny bauble
polished pebble
bit of sea glass
some old coin
or colored stone
forget about
everything else
pick up a thing
forget the pain
forget sadness
put it back down

Otherwise

I have many things
I need to type up,
and almost each day
I write still more.
I will never catch up,
since writing the things
is a lot more fun
then editing them.
They must be typed,
if they are meant
for public consumption.
Otherwise, I could
just leave them scribbled
on scraps of paper.
I would hire a "Cessna."
From high in the sky
I could send poems out,
so they would flutter down.
Hundreds of snowflakes,
pale blossom petals
adrift from a cherry tree,
and wounded white doves.

Winter work

That was some boring and cold job.
Scraping the layers of sheep grease
off all the pens in the shearing shed,
which was not in use that time of year.
Huge and drafty, gloomy and dark.
What passed on the sheep farm
for winter work, the scraper being
a triangle fabricated from steel,
welded crudely to a rough metal rod.
That thing caused some nasty blisters,
and my gloves had worn right through,
with nowhere to buy another pair.
I would just sit and scrape, scrape away.
For variety I might stand or kneel.
The task seemed to be never ending.
I'd wander around in my thoughts.
Shiver to try and make myself warmer.
Jump up and down, wiggle my toes
and look forward to "smoko" break.
Then lunch, tea, and finally knock off,
until starting again the following day.
Some jobs were not quite so bad.
Restoring old, dried paintbrushes.
Even chipping cement off salvaged bricks
so they could be used another time,
or pulling rusted nails from boards.
Though tedious, that work was better,
since I did it in the carpenter shop.
That place had a peat burning stove,
and wind would not whistle through it
in quite such a determined manner.

Welcome to California

I didn't expect a road that narrow.
East to west over mountain terrain.
Vertical rock on the left side,
sheer, precipice drop on the right.
With nothing resembling guardrails.
There were no roads like this back East.
Even in the Rockies, it wasn't so bad.
White knuckled, with both hands I'd grip
the wheel, negotiating all those turns
in my sixty-one Volkswagen van,
with a surfboard strapped to the roof.
Only three cylinders would function,
the fourth sacrificed to Mojave.
Of course, I was too broke to fix it.

Since I could barely make thirty-five,
I tried to select the slower, back roads.
This one was more like a goat path,
with almost enough width to meet
an oncoming, smallish vehicle,
but often not even that much room.
There was no place to turn around
though, in my terror I well may have,
so all I could do was keep driving.

Sensible people would not choose
to take such a steep and treacherous road,
that was barely a squiggle on a map.
Leave it up to a person like I was,
foolish and desperate, young and lost.
Yet stubborn enough to push on.
My old van might not keep pace
with traffic on the big interstates,
but I simply refused to give up.
As long as it didn't outright die,
I would make it to the Pacific,
and find myself in a perfect wave.

Would it

If there wasn't a God,
would everything still be
as beautiful as it is?

Would the sun rise and set
in such spectacularities?
Would crystal forms grow
out of both ice and rock,
to leave us in wonder?
Would autumn leaves change
into such glorious colors
shortly before they fall?
Would little children smile?
Would a wave curl over
in shimmers of turquoise?
Would the planets remain
set on their orbits and
the constellations too, would
they hang up above the sky
in myriads of diamonds?
This gentle breeze, would it waft
in, and would there be so many
species of plants and animals?
So many various kinds of
Stones, waters, and habitats,
weather, clouds and skies,
for all creation to enjoy?
Would I care so for you,
and you so care for me,
would any love even exist?

If there was not a God
would everything still be
as beautiful as it is?

Would it, would it, would it?

What a to do

I have so many things to do
but here I sit writing nonsense.
I have some phone calls to make.
I want to defrag the car,
and maintain the laptop.
Missing things need finding,
the house a disaster,
every room way too full.

It pretty much overwhelms me,
and therefore, I procrastinate.
The issues, however, do not go away,
I have noticed, strangely enough.

Nope, they usually get worse,
which makes them more daunting,
ever, then they were before.
So how do I tackle such matters?
I could look at it logically.
At least these ridiculous problems
give me something to write about.

Yet More

Is there anything more useless
than a pen that's out of ink?
This was once an excellent tool,
I am sure, but not anymore.
Now, though I press down in circles
nothing much happens, indents
on the paper is all it does.
It pays to have other pens around.
Even in distant hotel rooms,
with cars roaring by to somewhere,
and me in solitude writing
nonsense, using yet more ink.

Wisdom

This life is a crazy
what in the world.
We tolerate it
with wine or religion,
and anything we can find.
Cats do it much better.
They lie on the bed,
and soak more comfort
into their softness.
They worry not,
as long as mice run free,
the food dish is full,
and cicadas humm
in autumn darkness.

Arcadia

A temperate breeze
whispers upstream.
It trembles foliage
all new, fresh and soft.
Some pink lady slippers
nod at the passing,
and it cools my skin.
Peewees and vireos
lazily repeat the calls
that drift down from trees,
as I mosey my way
and pick along slow.
I step over twisted roots,
and around gray boulders,
decorated with lichen.
While water, all murmurs
and darks ripples by.
One neon, blue damselfly
fans its fine, black wings
on a mossy, damp rock.
As sunlight falls down,
falls dappling down.
Yellow, green, golden.

Words like

There was a writing guru,
who said I should never use
words like depression in my work.
A thing such as that should only
be implied was her point,
or perhaps not even that
maybe it must be denied.
The same way we do in life
if we behave acceptably.
We are only supposed to be well.
Like that gal sitting over there.
Her water bottle and salad meal.
So healthy and proper.
Perfect hair, and white blouse
without a smudge or spot on it.
She has that shiny, plastic jewelry,
and she is talking to her laptop.
Fall kick offs, inventory,
regional conference calls,
target stores, marketing trends.
Oh my lord, I feel certain
that gal is not in the least
acquainted with real depression.
That deep and unremitting kind,
that can take charge of a life.
Well I am willing to write it,
that word, and not deny it.

Cells of the monster

When does long become too long?
Does the human race seem old,
just because I am that way,
or is mankind now aged
past due retirement?
I don't mean each of us
as an individual person.
I refer to the species,
the being of it. We are but cells
of the monster, nothing more.
Did we learn all that we can,
invent more than enough stuff,
and explore far, far too much
already, is it time to quit?
Have we as an entire,
incredibly prolific,
massively multiplying entity
outlived our purpose?
And as for that purpose,
did anyone ever tell us,
more or less, what it was?

Worthwhile

likely there will not be
a worthwhile poem
not today anyway
my supply depleted
for a time at least
but this will soon change
these poems will conjure
themselves from something
without input from me
I cannot understand
how the thing occurs
but tomorrow perhaps
or sometime next week
I will sit down somewhere
find a pen that functions
and a poem will happen
lord willing of course
and the creek don't rise

Cobble

Stones don't talk so much, oh no.
Theirs is a mutter or murmur
perhaps a chatter, as water
swashes about them, a surge
of wasted wave, drawing on
back, down into the sea, but stones,
they know all about this thing
and discuss it among themselves.
Tides, swell, storms, heat and cold,
the very turning of the planet.
They understand such enigmas,
and might teach us quite a lot.
If only we could but understand, ah
that ancient wisdom of stones.

Wrens

A bird outside of my window
that day, loud, obnoxious,
as everything can seem to be
when my cat's not the darkest
thing around, when my mood
takes the award for that.
So I hissed at the window,
pssst, pssst, pssst, to scare
that feathered annoyance.
But it only hopped nearer
to me in that bush out there.
It, then another, yet one more,
an avian family perhaps.

Intrigued now, more than irked
I kept making that little noise
pushing air between my teeth,
while those three small, brown birds
took turns jumping to the screen.
Tiny feet clung to the wire
as they peered through the mesh,
curious, ever so inquisitive,
trying to locate that sound.
Wings aflutter, they twist their heads.
Rust colored back, short tails cocked,
rich, creamy fronted, thin billed.
A long, white eyebrow to highlight
a shining, minute bead of an eye.
I wanted to thank those three birds.
Each of them gave me reason to smile
on that day when I needed one.

Dearly dead

The place is so silent now.
Most of the flies dearly dead,
and gone at last, departed.
There's not a drone to be heard.
I know that one fly remains.
I saw it early this morning,
traversing the window pane.
But it was utterly quiet.
Perhaps it's the only one left
of what were multitudes,
until I eliminated them.
A veritable holocaust.

What a campaign it was.
One monstrous creature.
Earthbound, slow, heavy,
and vastly outnumbered
by a formidable force.
These quick, kinetic, tiny things
that freely dart, streaking through air,
and buzz to drive me crazy.
Yet watching that lone survivor,
now that the evil deed is done,
makes me feel a little sad.
Although I wanted to kill the flies,
I think I could rather miss them.

Wrong

What is life but long slow loss?
Is there anything else of meaning?
Gain, merely some bright illusion.
That toward which we work so hard.
A degree, a career, a family perhaps.
A creation of worth, achievement
of some kind but only a moment
of success. An ephemeral dream
which we never really realize.
It disintegrates or breaks apart,
lost to erosion, time and pain.
Or it decays and self destructs,
blowing away in gales and storm.
Leaving behind in its trailing wake
of wreckage and rust and ruin,
a human being stumbling along,
overwhelmed by the sadness of life.
Hurting and faltering, failed again,
and wondering what went so wrong.

Desires

If a person had their desires,
she might live in a home of stone
big enough for all of the stuff,
and with space to collect a bit more.

That house would be in a place
where owls and whippoorwills call,
frequently, if not every night,
and human neighbors are rather scarce.

If such a person should decide
to have yet one more fine adventure,
and go far away for awhile, she might
purchase a vehicle roomy enough
to live inside while she journeyed
about over all North America,
making her art and looking at birds.
It could be reckoned another big year.

When she returned to get older in
the gray stone house out in the woods,
she could sit and rock by the hearth.
Sipping a goblet of fine Merlot.
Contemplating the lives of seasons
or the wild red eye of a horned grebe,
while gently caressing which ever cat
happens to join her at that moment.

"Yankee"

It's dark out and cold,
shoveling this snow,
crusty on the drive.
A neighbor passes by
walking his yellow lab,
and we speak of things.
Bluebirds at a feeder,
a snowy owl irruption,
ice that will not be moved.
I pat his old pal gently
as it looks up tail awag,
pale and limping along
like a ghost dog in the night.

Falcon

Consider all the things
one could, perhaps have done,
but more than likely won't
ever take part in, not now.
No way in this go around.

I might have been a falconer
in a distant desert somewhere.
Turbaned and robed in dashiki.
My leather gauntlet protected hand
with a goshawk perched on it.
A bird to murmur softly to.

I would know its every feather,
the exact hue of the dark eye.
I could whisper love songs to it,
stroke its legs and folded wings,
touch its head, caress the back.

Then I'd fling that falcon aloft
in envy of its freedom of flight.
Exult as it soars, stoops, and kills,
shearing air with shriek and scream.
This feral and beautiful creature
free to wander the empty sky.
Yet it would return unto me,
to rest beneath a tasseled hood.
Chirrup and pip like a little child
that trusts me with its slumber.

Yellow Warbler

"Sweet- sweet -ever so sweet".
You may be one who suspects
the significance of those words,
if not used to simply describe
kittens, puppies, baby somethings,
and food that tastes far too good.
Or as random terms of endearment.
This not disregarding the fact,
that sweet is not a word I choose,
to describe my husband, and he
I am sure won't use it for me.
Indeed, I don't use it near enough.

Yet even in frigid February,
with two snowstorms every week,
I can recall sun on my skin,
and new leaves, green on the trees.
Aromas of apple and cherry blossoms
perfume the warm and soothing air,
when I walk through some lovely park.
I listen to refrains above me,
That rain down from the canopy.
"Sweet- sweet- ever so sweet",
a golden bird's song in the spring.

feline

contemplate having a cat about
just the idea of such a thing
to share place and love and life
with such an exquisite creature
yet she is ever a wild being
no matter how tame she sleeps
curled in tight unto herself
a warm and oval mound of purr
eyes concealed by one soft paw
tail wrapped close alongside her
the black gloss of her fur by far
the deepest dark in the room

As if

Out of control,
can we let go
for a moment?
No, we prepare
and plan ahead
for everything.
Think about it.
As if we make
a difference
in the long run.
As if the sea
will never rise.
As if the rocks
will never tell.
As if my cat
will never purr
again. As if
it all came from
some mistake, an
opportune and
auspicious bang.

Frog

That frog sits silent,
green and glistening.
So quiet in the sun
contemplating its world.
What does a frog think?
Crouched on a gray rock
at the edge of the water.
That glassy expanse spread
before it, liquid reflection.
Peace, solitude, stillness.
No thought of worry or stress.
Not of war, poverty, politics.
No concern with its looks,
or the cost of things.
Nor an increase in taxes, or
needed house renovations,
or a book it may not write.
What does that frog think?
Twenty minutes gone by now
and it is still crouched.
Like a cast thing, beauty
at the near edge of the lake.

A question of beauty

What would it be like
to be beautiful?
Long and lithe, with smooth, tan skin.
Lovely, thick hair, how would that feel?
People would acknowledge me then,
as I walked by them.
No more ignoring
or dismissive turning away.

Friends would come easy.

Women would get anxious
comparing themselves
to me, in worry I might outshine them.
Men would ogle at me,
and compete for my attention.
Yet I could just laugh,
secure in the fact,
that I will have plenty to choose from.

I could learn to like mirrors.

The nicest clothes would fit me,
and everything that I wore
would look simply wonderful
on my trim, and oh so hot, body.
I could drape myself.
Gracefully, languidly,
anywhere, and no one would mind in the least.
People would love me,
and want to be seen with me.

I wouldn't even need to be nice.

High tide

It's a high tide of humans,
covering this whole beach.
Towels, umbrellas, chairs,
and bodies, bodies, bodies.
Beautiful, and not quite so.
Young and old, big and small,
men and women and kids.
Various races and colors,
oiled with suntan lotion,
and smelling of coconut oil.

Music blares, children scream,
topless ladies turned face down.
Muscled guys in bikinied thongs,
Or surf trunks down to the knee.
People throwing balls around
and chasing after Frisbees.
Kids are running everywhere
and digging holes in the sand.

An old couple holding each other,
slowly walk with tentative steps,
and pick their way through masses,
along the edge of the ocean.
They just want to cool their feet,
not take their lives in their hands
on this hot, humid Saturday.

Bark

So I wandered around
an antique car show.
Lots of Fords, a few
Mercurys, Pontiacs,
a Cadillac Eldorado.
All were cherried out.
Chrome, high gloss paint,
except one ancient Ford
that boasted honest rust.
Fifties disco broadcast
loudly across the lot.
A form of forced gaiety,
and strangely, a kilted man
tried to drown out that stuff
with his lone set of pipes.

People sat by their cars,
looking fairly disgruntled.
Two leather jacketed types
with grease slick duck tails,
guardians of a Ford Mustang,
barked out loud as I passed.
Which commentary, I suspect,
was likely directed at me.
I did not however, respond.
I could see no reason
to acknowledge some guys
who speak the lingo of dogs,
even if they own cool cars.

Jump

She whispered a secret
the other evening,
misty eyed with Cabernet.
A compliment perhaps,
or an insult, who knows?

"When I think of jumping
I remember you."

Those words, enigmatic,
whatever could they mean?
She plays basketball,
or skips over a twirled rope?
Somehow I doubt it.
"When I think of jumping,"
off the bridge I suppose,
that high enough bridge
to her island home town.
But "I remember you," what
is she saying, I should
do this jumping business,
as I have more reason to?

Perhaps I simply understand
doing it, or maybe not
doing it, but wanting to.

Best we can do

We all have to find our way
to live with who we are.
Nobody claims it's easy
to love and respect us,
much less other humans.
It's all a part of being
alive in this space and time.

About the best we can do
is make peace with ourselves,
the people we encounter,
other living forms around us,
and in everything, honor
both the art and artisan.

Lost

Hey, psst, now that we are here,
can anybody tell me
where we were at before this?
It's rather an enigma
when memory fails us.

We guess this, postulate that,
heed the gurus and famous
others who may claim to know.
We read holy writ and word.
But still, if we are honest,
we must admit ignorance
on such important matters.

We will go somewhere as well,
some other where after this,
and that's another puzzle
that no one quite gets either.
Imagine being so lost.
Not knowing where we are from.
Not knowing where we are going.

Birds in color

rufus sided red necked
blue headed white eyed
yellow legs black backed
yes these are all birds
green tailed white winged
black capped blue footed
I have not seen that one
though I've heard tell of it
creepers and boobies are brown
I guess something had to be
and a most unfortunate tag
for a bird in my opinion
is Yellow Bellied Sapsucker
imagine being labeled that

Merg

There is a common merganser
in the river down behind "Phils".
Despite the name I can tell you this,
what birders call the common "merg",
is certainly not too plentiful,
at least not in these parts.
But I hope it is somewhere.
It is such an exquisite bird
and it did improve my mood.

I had been dark and gloomy.
Much like the weather that day,
as I grumped along icy sidewalks.
Doing my best not to slip and fall
between high piles of frozen slush,
I muttered my morbids to myself.
My back and hips were hurting.
Cold wind chilled my hands and face.
Yet some more snow in the forecast,
and my old car in the repair shop again.
All of this distressing minutia,
with a lovely duck down in the river,
to put it all into perspective.

Birds on bills

There is an owl on the dollar bill,
though one must look hard to find it.
I have no idea why it exists.
There is an eagle on it too,
but that bird is big and obvious,
and does not lead to questions.
People are everywhere today.
Going to the beach, crowding the roads,
rooting around in rummage sales.
Spending a lot of dollar bills.
I don't suppose many of them
think much about the eagle,
and as for the little owl,
they probably don't know it's there.

But it is.

Nights below twenty

On nights below twenty
in icy darkness of winter,
I must keep the heat on
at its lowest setting.
All faucets are left at a drip
so the pipes do not freeze.
There I am in the bed, awake
with my many blankets,
and one large, warm, black cat
that purrs alongside me.
I think of the tiny birds
out there in that bitter cold,
titmice, chickadees, wrens,
sparrows, kinglets all of them,
which do not migrate away,
so need endure frigid snaps.
One thought that soothes me
is the fact various birds
find a cavity somewhere.
A hole in an old tree,
or birdhouse not taken in,
like ones I have left out there.
Birds find such a small place
and stuff themselves into it.
As many of them as will fit to
fill the void with life and warmth
of soft, vibrant, feathered bodies.
Imagine them there in the dark.
This is such a comforting thought
it helps me to slip into sleep
on nights below twenty.

Bittern

Skulking denizen of the marshes,
a big bird, tall, with long, sharp bill.
It stands at water's edge,
swaying
in imitation of the reeds.
Striped brown and yellow,
Camouflaged, hidden,
to all but the most prying eyes.
There a pause,
a quick thrust and jab,
with that always so deadly bill.
Another frog,
one of eight downed
in the last forty minutes
I've sat, observing.
And now comes the good part.
I see the tip
of its pointed, pink tongue,
slip up one side of the long bill,
and down the other,
twice.
It did the same,
after every other frog it ate.
The satisfied bittern,
just licking its chops.

Orb

When I was a very young child,
too long ago to contemplate,
I watched an orb of blazing fire,
about the size of a large beachball.
I was all alone on a bearskin rug
working hard on my coloring.
That thing rolled in from the kitchen,
along the ceiling, and right across
the room, before it proceeded
out another door, down the hall,
always up high, out of my reach.

I don't remember being afraid,
simply curious, what was this
blinding white ball? I did not
sense any heat coming from it,
but it was incredibly bright
as it slowly tumbled along.

Somehow a star came inside
the house, I suppose I thought.
Well, I just sat there and watched that
star as it passed through the room.
Then I went back to my drawing.
A bit later on I remember, I wondered
why nobody would believe me,
when I tried to tell them about it.

Closing In

Cold November rain
windswept pelts down
splat on the windshield
as the wipers struggle
to clear it away enough
for me to notice those
hard little nuclei
formed of ice or snow
encased in every drop
a person could cry
but I do not suppose
it will do any good
an entire day in tears
with winter closing in

Bumble

they are so big
and bumbly
I step outside
of my front door
they drone around
I am not sure
if they can sting
but they can drill
quite well in wood
up under eaves
perfectly round
smallish holes
just the right size
for fat bodies
yellow and black
fuzzy and striped
to fit into
carpenter bees
I do not know
if they are scarce
or endangered
like other bees
some people claim
I should kill them
they cause damage
but I will not
they do their thing
every summer
being a bee
and as for me
I let them be

Patient persistence

The male warbler sings
his short, plaintive song
over and over again, with
such patient persistence,
here in this wooded place.
I can see him up there,
high in a new, leafed tree.
He throws his head back
for each trill and buzz.
Small, bright, golden body,
stretched so, vibrating
with effort every time.
I wish I could respond
but he is not calling for me.
He's trying to find a mate,
and nobody is answering.
I sure hope someone will.

Tundra

Once in a far and northern place
a wanderer sat for a time,
on a lichen covered, granite rock.
Wearied from a hard, steep trek
around and over the island.
Such a vast, inspiring view
demanded appreciation.
Stark, gray, windswept beauty.

Right then, in some spirit way
a raven appeared, unbidden,
and hovered for several moments,
not even three feet from her face.
Powerful, glossy, mysterious,
with a far, all seeing dark eye,
a remarkable, large black bird.

She reached a hand out timid, awed,
and it landed on the ground nearby.
They contemplated each other,
that wanderer and that bird,
then went their separate ways.
Touched by another vagabond
soul lost in a barren world.

Daunt

There's thousands of books
in this gigantic store.
Millions of words
are printed on pages.
One might imagine
that it all has been done.
Everything's
been published by now.
Some real audacity
would be required,
if one were to think
they had a new thing
worth writing about.

Seeing

Who are you, what are you thinking in there?
Your green eyes give me almost nothing.
But as they meet mine a moment, I smile,
though how would I know if you're smiling back?
All I can see is your turning away.
Am I infidel then, am I an enemy,
with my face, my hair, and my arms exposed?
Do I only represent sin and evil,
instead of simply an alternate culture,
with some different customs, beliefs, or creed?

I would so like to sit awhile with you,
converse if we could, maybe drink some nice tea.
I would get to know you perhaps, just a little.
We might tell each other something about
how it's been living in our diverse worlds.
Our dreams and joys, our woes and fears.
But I don't know if you would actually want that,
and, I'm somewhat reluctant to admit,
I feel a little anxious about offending you.
So we will be going our separate ways,
and our lives will be the lesser for it.
Oh woman beneath that concealing veil,
there is no way I ever can prove this so,
but somehow, I know you are beautiful.

Time Gone

There is a thing one may come to know,
the blessed dignity of silence.
After the great party is over
and the revelers have all gone home.
When dreaming stages are almost done,
and only the deepest sleep remains.
When a last, dried leaf falls from the tree,
and winter sets in to have its day.
Frail hands caress thinning, gray hair,
yet tremble with this tiny effort.
Ambitious plans of youth are folded
and placed away neatly in time gone.

Drawing

Dogtown, it draws me
its whispers and ears
among the erratics.
Moraine boulders, granite,
left by laurentide ice.

I would drive there I guess,
it isn't all that far.

Stone walls, cellar holes,
the only indicators
anyone called it home,
other than spirits, witches,
voices, and ancient stirs.
Twisted brush, rock dolmens,
crawling blueberry bushes.
Broken glass underfoot,
forlorn, burnt out cars,
abandoned ephemera
to litter the landscape.

And the form of a face
pressed down into clay.

Suffocation, murder,
solid evidence
forever cast there.
One more solitary
drawn into Dogtown.

Eternally empty

Nothing will come.
She sits staring at fresh, new paper,
pen in hand, ready, waiting.
Expectant even,
but nothing appears.
She only sees marks that are already there.
Twenty-seven lines across the page,
thin, blue, horizontal, mocking,
and one more hanging on the margin,
long, red, vertical, derisive.
She sits and stares.
The lines start moving,
shifting, merging, weaving together,
blurring, and finally fading away,
until they don't exist,
anywhere at all,
to her weary eyes,
glazed now and clouded.
The page is empty.
Absolutely and eternally empty.
As such it becomes intolerable.
She turns to look out the window.
More of that snow is drifting down.
Big, cold, wet flakes.
Impossibly white.
Dismal and bleak as her mood these days.
Loathing herself, a single tear falls.
The blot makes a new kind of mark on the page.
She crumples it then, throwing it down,
and stumbles out into the storm.

the sad days

Would you like
to know me
i cannot
imagine
why you would
i am sad
and messed up
i'm depressed
the sun sets
out there now
and i won't
get involved
it goes down
with no help
from me none
and i shan't
go outdoors
i will not
even look
at the night
and winter
returning
chill within
and without
dark inside
and outside
would you like
to know me
i cannot
imagine
why you would

Heavy pet

It seems a tad ridiculous
to write yet another thing
about felines I have known.
Yet how is it, I wonder today,
that the largest and heaviest,
is also the most particular,
when it comes to what she eats?
One would think such fuss budgets
might be delicate and thin,
but that appears to be wrong.
This one just sniffs at her food,
it's the expensive brand too,
and turns a black nose up to it.
Then it's the action with claws,
scritch, scritch around the dish,
all around, a thorough job,
picking away at an empty floor.
She will work for several minutes.
My best guess is she reckons
that she's burying the stuff.
She is smart enough otherwise.
It is just that she has a strange
relationship with her food.
Yet, one would never suspect it
if they were to see that fat creature,
or attempt to carry the heavy pet.

Projecting

Sorry, I'm really projecting here,
my fears, and woes, and grim obsessions.
Some people try to write out the pain.
Scrawling their words onto the pages,
hoping, somehow, that will make some room
inside of them, for healing and light.

This morning I watched a tiny bird.
Hopping around, it picked at snow.
I saw a tree, strong, brave in the wind,
with limbs upraised in constant homage.
At home I heard my cat in full purr,
curled beside me, soft, safe, and warm.
An owl spoke out of the darkness,
Solitary, so cold in the night.

So what am I to do with this life?
Shall I try and learn from all of these?
Instad of just finding a place to hide,
and comfort myself till it's over.

Shattered

Looking through a shattered window
I see you distorted
fractured into tiny shards
bright and glittering
full of light and color
trying desperately
to hold
together
you imagine you still look strong
but you are fragile
ready to fall apart
hundreds of little
pieces complicated
and so beautiful
but so
broken

Thy

if it be Thy will
what about mine
where does my will
fit into this equation
i would like to be well
i want to know less pain
do these facts matter
and if so then how
what is this existence
but long and slow loss
for the fortunate
and for lots of people
it comes much faster
what recourse have we
are we to be passive
to humbly bow our head,
are we to kneel down
hands clasped in prayer
to receive our sentence
all to your glory eh
no matter what it be
no matter how it hurts
if it be Thy will

Insomnia

Last night I could not sleep.
I yearned to go outside the house
into the dark yard, hidden,
and lie flat out on my back.
Naked on the wet, spring grass.
Arms, legs spread out to greet
a soft fall of gentle rain.
The drops could trace all along
my body's mounds and wrinkles.
Collect in the hollow places.
Cool water, moist and sweet.
My pale skin might drink it in,
and be some comforted for it.
Then I'm sure I could have slept.

Katrina

Because He lives, we live it says.
Eternity is our reality.
OK, I try to believe it.
I try to believe that this is not
all, that in all, there is.
But it's hard, Lord, I say it's hard.
This world is a sad place, a bad,
and underneath a southern sky
the water is some ninety degrees,
perfect for fueling hurricanes
that blow in destruction and fear.
Tidal surges thirty- five feet
in a town of around altitude ten.
No highland in Mississippi.

Clinging on to a massive live oak,
one, maybe two, can hang in there.
Lord tell me why, tell me why.

Death floods in with the gulf
and inundates the cathedral.
It flushes out pews and alter
leaving behind an empty shell.
Glorious, stained glass art intact,
everything else inside gone.
A survivor looks up and prays,
"Lord you sure put the hurtin' to it,"
but nobody understands why,
Lord, nobody really knows why.

Turtle Hill

My niece sits in a canoe
struggling with a paddle,
in true determination.
A little girl, short hair,
blue top, and matching shorts.
Working hard to learn
wiles and ways of small boats.

She's tethered by a long rope
from the stern to a cleat
on the dock down at the lake.
She's not going to drift away.

So smooth, all is reflection,
as a family sits and talks.
Murmuring voices in beauty.
Dangle of feet off the dock
to ripple all that smooth glass.

The slap at an odd mosquito
as distant thunder growls
far out across the water.

Laurel

She almost missed the laurel
this first time in a long time.
Caught up in other things
cats, buttons, poetry, madness,
whatever. Just other things.
Yet laurel bloomed, regardless.
Glorious clouds along the road,
nearly gone by, but she saw it.
That measure of passing season,
and ever ephemeral beauty.
Another year sliding away.

The Best Answer

But why?
There are so many questions.
All the gigantic conundrums.
The puzzles, mysteries, riddles,
enigmas and dilemmas.
Sure we can work for lifetimes
with our formulas and experiments,
our academic qualifications, our
scientific analysis, our hubris and
pride of intellectual genius.
We can use the biggest mainframes
that IBM manufactures. However,
the best answer may turn out to be,
Why not?

I mean like lost

Have you ever
misplaced yourself?
I mean, like lost
this thing called you.
So look around.
Search here and there.
Call up a friend
to ask if they
know where you're at.
They likely won't.
You might want to call the cops.
Report you are
a person who's
missing again.
Yet I'm not sure
I'd advise that.
You could end up
finding yourself
locked in a place
with no way out.

Weeds

Some weeds simply defy me,
attached as they are to a rope
of long and slippery, sinewy root.
I yank them up again and again,
but the deep, strong root remains,
and sends new shoots up rapidly.

Other weeds have these taproots
like dandelions, deeply probing
way, way down into the soil.
I pull them up carefully, and slow,
but if even a tiny piece remains
of that tap, the plant grows again.

Then there are those fragile weeds
that break off easily at the stem,
and separate away from the root.
They're not in the least discouraged
by this seeming destruction.
They replicate fast, without fail.

So when I am down on my knees,
I do battle with these growing things
in the dirt, to maintain a garden.
I can entertain myself moseying,
meandering around with my musings.
They help the hours to pass on by.

Sometimes I'll find myself wishing
I had the grit, the power, the strength,
and even half the resilience that
these plentiful plants possess.
Such a defiant will to survive.
The sheer tenacity of a weed.

Weary

This cat loves its belly massaged.
I wonder if Che is home or not?
It must be light, not temperature.

I'm sure there were others as well,
that escaped without recognition.

All of them in addition to
scraps and remnants of dreams,
and poems trying to happen.

None of this is of interest,
except for the remarkably
simultaneous nature
of these varied ruminations,
and frankly, disconnected thoughts.

Assuming this goes on all day,
it is fairly understandable,
and not the least surprising
that my mind gets rather weary.

Rock and weed

If I swim out far enough,
I come to the rock and weed.
Thousands of heart shaped leaves
in a wonderful shade of green,
with long, thin, red, snake like stems.
I can spread them apart before me,
my stretched arms sweep them aside
so they brush along my body.
The soft sensation on my skin,
like multitudes of gentle fingers
that stroke and caress me with love.

Dragon flies circle around my head
so iridescent and brilliant,
in cinnabar reds and glowing blues.
They rest on lily pad thrones,
rise and hover as I draw near,
then zip off on odonata missions.

Finally, I can see the rock
in my nearsighted myopia.
Yes, sure enough there are turtles,
that slip in with a modest sploosh.
They'll join me on this warm August day
in a blissfully cool, glass calm lake.

The ruined tower

It was a magnificent edifice
when new, I would imagine.
A mad architects finest
and ultimate creation.
I know not when, or where it was.
Maybe some Victorian fantasy,
maybe the tower of Babel.
I am sure though, I dwelt there once.
Perhaps a part of me never left.

After time had destroyed it,
on the bottom floor, some rooms
still remained as apartments.
Someone collected a bit of rent
from destitute, edge people.
Kind of a dubious artist's lair,
quite illegal, way below code.

The tower above, what still stood
of it, swayed precariously.
Stark, massive, a framework
in gusty weather, much too high
and dangerous to demolish.
Years would need to finish the task
of returning it all to the earth.
A beautiful, fragile ruin.

Ah, but if a person dared,
and had the agility required,
they could climb up, and rise among
the abandoned heights of the thing.
Sections of stairways and ladders.
Pigeons cooing and strutting proud.
Forbidden rooms with sagging floors,
moldy mattresses and blankets.
There I could sleep and hide away,
comforted by my loneliness,

where others would never find me.

Sometimes I might discover
forgotten treasures and artifacts,
lurking in corners and crannies.
A few times I gathered the nerve,
for sure a perilous prospect.
Yet when I crept near the edge
I would get a most breathtaking view.
Now all that I needed to do
was step off to fly forever,
and cast my sadness unto the wind.

Tree and grass

In the field a stately tree
felt ever so strong and proud.
The tallest entity around, it was
admired by all who saw it.
The tree boasted to the grasses
that cowered around its massive trunk,
"Look at you there, pathetic, small,
puny and weak, I bet that you
bow down to every tiny breeze.
But I stand straight, defiant, great,
and nothing will ever bend me.
Nobody notices you down there
but everyone will look my way.
Don't you wish that you were me?"

The grasses however were silent,
thoughtful, but not too ashamed.
They simply tried to understand.
The tree had not grown only big,
but somewhat swollen with pride,
and it likely wouldn't care to know
what something so small would think.
The grass therefore, kept its peace.
It continued to bend and sway
in response to the waves of wind.

A storm came through one day,
as storms inevitably will.
It was nearly a hurricane,
so long and hard did it blow.
The tree resisted quite awhile,
standing strong, it creaked and groaned,
but finally cracked, broke and fell.
As it lay there it whispered,
"how grasses do you still stand?"

"Ah," said the grasses sorrowfully,
sad to see the great one brought low.
"We have just chosen not to fight
the gales and storms of this life,
and we've learned to bend with the wind."

Hitching

No one would pick her up that day.
It was cold, wet, getting dark
along the big busy interstate
Not heavy rain, that light misty kind
that can chill you down to the bone,
and nobody was stopping for her.

What was was she going to do, she knew
she wouldn't get a ride in the night.
No buildings were around here.
A chain link fence prevented her
from reaching the woods, and forest
creatures from reaching the road.

She looked around herself in dismay.
There, on the fence, a tarp,
An old plastic sheet snagged on wire.
Dirty and wet, shredded and holed,
but it might be better than nothing.
Freeing the thing, she bundled it up,
and ran with it across to the zone,
between lanes of speeding traffic,
those two lanes south, two lanes north.

The median of separation was
an alarmingly narrow piece of land
but it did have some vegetation
that she could perhaps crawl into.
What other option did she have?
So there she lay wound in that tarp
like a sad and abandoned mummy,
all that long night, shivering wet,
as trickles of cold found her skin.

Anxious, wide eyed, sleep did not come,
as card and trucks roared by blind.
Big tires screamed on wet pavement

Engines growled and rubber slapped
north and southbound in the dark.
Much too close to where she cringed.

She wondered where she'd lost her way.
Everyone else was going somewhere else,
that had to be better than where she was.

Eventually a gray dawn came.
She crawled out of her precarious lair,
stiff, staggered back across the lanes,
and stood in her old spot hungry, cold,
pathetic, lost, discouraged, disheveled.
She needed to hope, despite the odds
that somehow, someway, somebody
would open their heart just a little bit,
slow down, stop, and give her a ride.

Realm

"Southern ocean" merely words,
that don't mean much to most of us.
Yet they are so significant
to those who have known the long way.
The realm of the albatross,
that hallowed, great, winged bird.
Aloof and proud, fierce of eye,
and one whose consent was required,
if I were to make safe passage.

All too well, I still can recall
that tiny boat with shortened sail,
ever so slowly struggling, staggering
through an infinity of waters.
Their very wrinkled, shining surface,
like some titan's crumpled, silver foil.
This expanse of hard and massive waves,
somehow so awfully vaster,
than lesser, warmer, and calmer seas,
of lower, more temperate latitudes.

So many hours alone at the helm
in those endless, late, night watches.
Steering under the Southern Cross,
uncountable stars above me,
liquid, green fire sparking below,
cold phosphorescence.
Yet no lights from other vessels,
there were no other boats out there.

Shivering in the frigid night
I could listen to all the voices.
The crying of lonely waters,
the moaning of lost sailors,
the song and whispering in my mind,
and the laughter of gigantic birds.

About the Author

Kathy Kroener does not have degrees nor fancy awards worth mentioning, none the less, she has lived a full life, helped by her grit and determination. She has sailed oceans, explored the tundra, and lived on an island alone, she's paddled to icebergs, lived through a war, and has ridden thousands of waves. Kathy's been homeless, lost and sick. No trust fund baby her, she left home early, was lonely and broke, and is well acquainted with pain. Yet somehow she has survived the years to experience these things, and more, and through it all she has sought the light, while willing to face the darkness.

She lives with her husband, George, and a substantial black feline named the Splendid Dark Beauty.

Kathy has been a visual artist for a long time and has been a voracious reader for as long as she can remember. In more recent years she's discovered the joy of writing. Her husband claims that "It's like turning on a faucet. The stuff just pours out."

Kathy writes the things she knows, tapping into her large reservoir of experience. She is working on a book about her life, but has found that poetry is where her heart really lies. These days Katherine is also an avid birder, as always, finding her solace in nature.